HENRY FIELDING

from a sketch by HOGARTH *used as a frontispiece to Fielding's Works, 1762*

FIELDING

by JOHN BUTT

PUBLISHED FOR
THE BRITISH COUNCIL
and the NATIONAL BOOK LEAGUE
BY LONGMANS, GREEN & CO., LONDON, NEW YORK, TORONTO

LONGMANS, GREEN & CO. LTD.
6 & 7 Clifford Street, London W.1
Also at Melbourne and Cape Town

LONGMANS, GREEN & CO. INC.
55 Fifth Avenue, New York 3

LONGMANS, GREEN & CO.
215 Victoria Street, Toronto 1

ORIENT LONGMANS LTD.
Bombay, Calcutta, Madras

First published in 1954

B55- 00997

Printed in Great Britain by Benham and Company Limited
Colchester

FIELDING

I

To say that the English novel began in the seventeen-forties with the work of Richardson and Fielding is to invite refinement, if not contradiction. The Elizabethans had plenty of novels to read, by Nashe, Greene, Lodge, and Deloney; in the latter half of the seventeenth century there were numerous translations and imitations of the French romance ; and Mrs. Behn, Defoe, and Mrs. Manley have all some claims upon the historian of the novel. Yet there is something in the broad contention which Richardson and Fielding, for all their differences, would have approved. Recalling the circumstances of his writing *Pamela* (1740) Richardson claimed, in a letter to a friend, that he had hit upon ' a new species of writing ', and Fielding was equally confident that *Joseph Andrews* (1742) was a ' kind of writing, which I do not remember to have seen hitherto attempted in our language '. At least some of their readers were prepared to acknowledge the claim. Dr. Johnson, writing in 1750, when *Clarissa*, *Tom Jones*, and Smollett's *Roderick Random* had also been published, was able to distinguish one important difference between the new style of fiction and the old. In *Rambler* No. 4, he remarks that:

> The works of fiction, with which the present generation seems more particularly delighted, are such as exhibit life in its true state, diversified only by accidents that daily happen in the world, and influenced by passions and qualities which are really to be found in conversing with mankind. . . . Its province is to bring about natural events by easy means, and to keep up curiosity without the help of wonder : it is therefore precluded from the machines and expedients of the heroick romance, and can neither employ giants to snatch away a lady from the nuptial rites, nor knights to bring her back from captivity ; it can neither bewilder its personages in deserts, nor lodge them in imaginary castles.

Such, Johnson would have us believe, were the themes and

incidents of the older style of fiction. All the writer had to do was to ' let loose his invention, and heat his mind with incredibilities ; a book was thus produced without fear of criticism, without the toil of study, without knowledge of nature, or acquaintance with life '. Very different, in Johnson's opinion, was the equipment of the modern novelist. Besides ' learning which is to be gained from books ', he must have ' experience which . . . must arise from general converse and accurate observation of the living world '; his books will then be not merely ' just copies of human manners ', but they will also serve as ' lectures of conduct, and introductions into life '.

Perhaps Johnson was not altogether fair to the older style of fiction. Many novelists from the time of Sidney onwards had been interested in providing ' lectures of conduct '; and many besides Defoe (whom Johnson seems to have overlooked) were acquainted with life. But one of the principal differences between the old and the new he has made very clear in his emphasis upon ' accidents that daily happen in the world ': the men and women in the novels of Fielding—and Richardson—act ' in such scenes of the universal drama as may be the lot of any other man ' or woman. That is true of neither Sidney nor Defoe. A young man might imagine himself feeling like Sidney's Musidorus or acting like Robinson Crusoe ; but he could never expect to share their experiences, as he might expect to share the experiences of Tom Jones. A young woman might well believe all that Moll Flanders reports had happened to her ; but she could scarcely say of Moll, as she could say of Amelia or even of Clarissa, ' there but for the grace of God go I '.

But when Fielding, Richardson, and Johnson insisted that such accidents as ' daily happen in the world ' must be the staple of the new style of fiction, they were writing not at the beginning but towards the end of a critical tradition. The marvellous had long been losing in esteem, and writers of romances in the previous century had been accustomed to discuss in their prefaces to what use historical incidents

might be put. Thus Sir George Mackenzie, in the preface
to his *Aretina* (1660), had censured those who have ' stuffed
their Books with things impracticable, which because they
were above the reach of mans power, they should never
have fallen within the circle of his observation '; and Robert
Boyle took credit for having chosen an episode from history
for his *Theodora* (1687), since:

> True Examples do arm and fortify the mind far more effica-
> ciously, than Imaginary or Fictitious ones can do; and the
> fabulous labours of *Hercules*, and Exploits of *Arthur* of *Britain*,
> will never make men aspire to Heroick Vertue half so power-
> fully, as the real Examples of Courage and Gallantry afforded
> by *Jonathan*, *Cæsar*, or the *Black Prince*.

These novelists were following in the steps of de Scudéry,
the most famous of the French romance writers, whose
Ibrahim (1641) had been translated into English in 1652. In
the preface to that work de Scudéry claimed that he had
observed

> the Manners, Customs, Religions, and Inclinations of People:
> and to give a more true resemblance to things, I have made the
> foundations of my work Historical, my principal Personages
> such as are marked out in the true History for illustrious
> persons.

Even though the practice of these writers did not always
accord with their theory, it is easy to see how in time the
desire for ' a more true resemblance to things ' could lead
the author of *Robinson Crusoe* to declare that ' the Editor
believes the thing to be a just History of Fact ; neither is
there any Appearance of Fiction in it '. The innocent deception of passing off fiction as history or biography is per-
petrated in several title-pages. Thus the reader is offered
*The Life and Strange Surprising Adventures of Robinson
Crusoe, of York, Mariner. Written by Himself*, or *The Fortunes
and Misfortunes of the Famous Moll Flanders. Who was Born
in Newgate, was Twelve Year a Thief, Eight Year a Transported*

Felon in Virginia. Written from her Memorandums. Twenty
years later the novelists were less concerned for the success
of their deceptions. *Pamela, or Virtue Rewarded* is merely *A
narrative which has its foundations in Truth and Nature* ; but
the tradition of offering ' a more true resemblance to
things ' is maintained in such titles as *The History of the
Adventures of Joseph Andrews and of his friend Mr. Abraham
Adams ; Clarissa. Or, The History of a Young Lady ; The
History of Tom Jones, a Foundling.*

In choosing to let their novels pass as histories or bio-
graphies, these writers were aware of what they might adopt
in structure and narrative technique from a well-established
literary ' kind ', and it is not surprising that they should
search for profitable analogies in other forms of narrative
as well. It was certainly to be expected that they would
have an eye to the epic in particular, since this was a form
of paramount reputation and one to the analysis of whose
constituent parts much critical thought had been given.
Sidney had long ago declared that the *Theagenes and Cariclea*
of Heliodorus was not prevented from exerting influence as
an heroic poem though it was written in prose, and he had set
an example when revising his *Arcadia* to make its structure
conform more truly to epic principles. De Scudéry again
had emphasized what valuable lessons a novelist might learn
from the epic, and possibly the most successful of modern
epics, Fénelon's *Les Aventures de Télémaque*, had been written
in prose. Thus when Fielding told his readers that *Joseph
Andrews* was to be regarded as ' a comic epic poem in
prose ' and that this, moreover, was a ' kind of writing
which I do not remember to have seen hitherto attempted
in our language ', the novelty of his claim lay not so much
in the notion of a prose epic, nor even of a comic epic
poem—for this everyone recognised in Pope's *Dunciad*—
but in a conflation of the two. And though the act of
conflation required the spark of Fielding's genius, the critical
temper of the day was prepared to see such a spark fly.

II

Fielding himself was also well prepared for this new venture by his experience of men and books, and by his previous career as a writer. He came of a family of small landowners in the West Country related to the Earls of Denbigh : amongst his immediate forebears we find men who had risen to positions of some distinction in the learned professions. It might be suspected that the novelist derived his inclination towards the law from his mother's father, who was a Justice of the Queen's Bench, and that to his paternal grandfather, an archdeacon of Salisbury, he owed both his love of learning and the strong bent towards Christian moral teaching which characterize his novels. Though we need not pay too much attention to such surmises nor enquire what traits of character were inherited from his somewhat feckless father, Lieutenant-General Edmund Fielding, it is at least clear in what rank of society he was bred.

After a boyhood spent on his mother's Dorsetshire estates he joined his father in London, and in 1728, at the early age of twenty-one, he wrote his first play, *Love in Several Masques*, a comedy of manners. Partly no doubt owing to the patronage of his cousin, Lady Mary Wortley Montagu, the play was performed at Drury Lane Theatre, and ran for four nights. But though he was to lead a busy life as a dramatist and theatre-manager between 1730 and 1737, Fielding now decided not to pursue his moderate success but to enrol as a student in the Faculty of Letters at the University of Leyden under the redoubtable critic Peter Burmann. In later years he was to mock Burmann's editorial manner in the notes to his burlesque tragedy *Tom Thumb* ; but it is probable that he now received his first instructions in critical theory, and began to obtain his extensive knowledge of classical literature. Certainly he was later to own a remarkable library of classical and modern texts ; and his novels show that he possessed what Johnson considered the primary equipment of the modern novelist, ' learning which is to be gained from books '.

At the age of thirty-five when he began to write *Joseph Andrews*, he had had sufficient opportunity to acquire the second item in Johnson's equipment, ' experience which . . . must arise from general converse and accurate observation of the living world '. If we did not know this from *Joseph Andrews* itself, we should know it from the plays written during the seven years following his return from Leyden in 1730 and from his journalistic essays. These serve to show something of the range of that experience as well as indicating how the experience might be used by the future novelist.

Writing for the stage had taught him how to manipulate dialogue and to devise speech rhythms for distinguishing a country squire from a man-about-town or a modish lady from a young miss. It had taught him to contrive a concatenation of incidents by which the principal characters are brought together in the final scene of play or novel for the unravelling of the knot. It seems also to have accustomed him to imagine some of his scenes in terms of a drawing-room set on a stage of limited dimensions, and to offer in the novel scenes which experience told him would be effective in the theatre. His plays abound in scenes where characters are interrupted by an unexpected entry which disturbs and perplexes their existing relationship. Thus in Act III of *The Temple Beau* (1730), an early play, young Wilding is pretending to make love to Lady Lucy Pedant and has just taken her in his arms when they are interrupted by the entry first of her husband (' Hoity-toity? Hey-day ! What's here to do ? Have I caught you, gentlefolks. . . ') and, immediately after, of Wilding's father, who has lately discovered his son's deceptions. This use of the unexpected entry is more skilfully developed in *Tom Jones* (XV, 5), in a scene where Lord Fellamar's unwanted attentions to Sophia in Lady Bellaston's house are interrupted by the entry of Squire Western, who has at last discovered where

Sophia has taken refuge. Western is followed by Lady
Bellaston, who joins him in representing to Sophia the ad-
vantages of agreeing to a proposal of marriage. Lord
Fellamar, being assured that he was meant by Lady Bellaston
and assuming that he must also be meant by Western,
decides to take advantage of the new turn in the situation:

> Coming up therefore to the squire, he said, 'Though I
> have not the honour, sir, of being personally known to you;
> yet, as I find I have the happiness to have my proposals accepted,
> let me intercede, sir, in behalf of the young lady, that she may
> not be more solicited at this time.'
> 'You intercede, sir!' said the squire; 'why, who the
> devil are you?'
> 'Sir, I am Lord Fellamar,' answered he, 'and am the happy
> man, whom I hope you have done the honour of accepting
> for a son-in-law.'
> 'You are the son of a b——,' replied the squire, 'for all
> your laced coat. You my son-in-law, and be d——n'd
> to you!'
> 'I shall take more from you, sir, than from any man,'
> answered the lord; 'but I must inform you, that I am not
> used to hear such language without resentment.'
> 'Resent my a——', quoth the squire. 'Don't think I am
> afraid of such a fellow as thee art! because hast got a spit there
> dangling at thy side. Lay by your spit, and I'll give thee
> enough of meddling with what doth not belong to thee. I'll
> teach you to father-in-law me. I'll lick thy jacket.'
> 'It's very well, sir,' said my lord, 'I shall make no distur-
> bance before the ladies. I am very well satisfied. Your
> humble servant, sir; Lady Bellaston, your most obedient.'

There can be little doubt that in this episode Fielding has
made use of his theatrical experience, as he has also done in
scenes involving the use of stage properties, even though the
number of these is meagre. The most notable example in
his plays is perhaps to be found in Act III of *The Letter
Writers* (1731), where Mrs. Wisdom and her gallant Rakel
are disturbed by the arrival of Mrs. Softly, and Rakel,
tender of Mrs. Wisdom's reputation, hides under the table.

Mrs. Softly is followed by Mr. Wisdom and a nephew, who in a drunken fit overturns the table, and discovers Rakel. This is the prototype of more memorable discoveries, of Lady Bellaston discovering Mrs. Honour in hiding behind the bed in Jones's room (XV, 7), and of Jones discovering the philosopher Square behind a rug in Molly Seagrim's bed-chamber (V, 5). It is surprising that after his early experiment in *The Letter Writers* Fielding should not have improved upon the device in a subsequent play. The hint was to be taken by Sheridan, however, who shows, in the scene of Lady Teazle's discovery behind a screen in Joseph Surface's room, that he had learned something from each of the episodes in *Tom Jones*, for he there combined both the embarrassment of Square's discovery and the reversal of fortune which sprang from Mrs. Honour's.

During his career as a dramatist Fielding had attempted a considerable number of forms. He had written witty comedies of intrigue in the Restoration manner, farces, ballad operas with political implications, burlesques, comedies reflecting upon modern manners, and satirical comedies on the pattern of Buckingham's *Rehearsal* in which an absurd play is rehearsed with comments from the author, a critical acquaintance, and the players. Two of the last of these, *Pasquin* (1736) and *The Historical Register* (1737), were amongst the most successful of his plays, and the device which he there employs of accompanying the action with critical comment from the wings may perhaps have suggested to him the ' prolegomenous ' chapters of *Tom Jones* which, on a more serious level, serve the same purpose. Equally significant is his early experience of burlesque in *Tom Thumb* (1730) and *The Covent-Garden Tragedy* (1731), where by burlesquing an old-fashioned ' kind ', he produced a new ' kind ', as it were, by mutation. Though the burlesque of epic is not so prominent in *Joseph Andrews* and its successors as the burlesque of tragedy in *Tom Thumb*, it is by a similar process of ' mutation ' that the novels arose.

Fielding's experience as a journalist was scarcely less useful to his future career than his experience in the theatre. From 1739 to 1741 he was the leader of a group of writers responsible for conducting an Opposition newspaper called *The Champion*. To this journal Fielding contributed a number of essays modelled on *The Spectator*. Just as Addison had invented a Spectator Club and had defined the *persona* of one member of the club who should write his lucubrations, aided and abetted by his fellow-members, so Fielding assumed the *persona* of Captain Hercules Vinegar, whose business it was to write about the issues of the day, aided by his wife Joan and their two sons. Like Addison, too, he varies the form of his articles, now character sketches, now lay sermons, or letters from imaginary correspondents, visions, critical papers, essays in instalments, and Saturday papers on religious matters. These essays reveal a more serious-minded Fielding than we might have supposed judging from the plays alone. Here he is to be seen formulating his views on the moral problems which form the staple of his three novels, and illustrating those problems by anecdotes and character sketches. He was also unwittingly practising himself in what was regarded as an important part of the novelist's duty. The novelist was expected to provide, in Johnson's phrase, ' lectures of conduct '. He was not merely to edify by the story he told, but to make sure that his lesson was understood. Hence the pithy, and summary comment upon manners, common alike to the novelist and the essayist.

III

For much of his future work Fielding was well prepared both in theory and in practice. It is not surprising, therefore, that from the beginning his command was assured, even though his approach was haphazard, even accidental. If it had not been for Richardson's *Pamela*, he might never have become a novelist. This story deals with a young woman's marriage outside her station in life. When a

young man and a young woman of different social classes
fell in love, it was generally assumed that their association
could only be illegitimate. ' Why, what is all this, my
dear,' said Sir Simon Darnford, one of Richardson's characters, to his wife, ' but that our neighbour has a mind to his
mother's waiting maid ! And if he takes care she wants for
nothing, I don't see any great injury will be done her. He
hurts no *family* by this.' And Parson Williams reports the
opinion of Parson Peters that this was ' too common and
fashionable a case to be withstood by a private clergyman
or two '. What made this particular case uncommon was
that Pamela resists her would-be seducer, yet cannot help
loving him in spite of his ill-treatment ; and that Mr. B.
expects to be able to seduce Pamela, yet, in spite of favour-
able circumstances, he is won by her behaviour and against
the opinion of the world to offer her marriage.

Thus Pamela's Virtue is Rewarded. But though Richardson emphasizes that aspect of his story in his sub-title, there
is much more to the novel. Had that been all, we might
have expected that her virtue would be rewarded by
marriage in the last chapter. But the ceremony takes place
two-thirds of the way through ; and yet we read on, since
it is not merely Pamela's chastity but the integrity of her
personality which is tested. She must also be shown pre-
serving in her new station her humility, her thankfulness,
her piety, and her intelligence. Hers is indeed a most
difficult task. She is required to loathe Mr. B's behaviour,
and yet to love him ; to be content with her lowly posit-
ion, yet to aspire to Mr. B's hand ; to be humble, yet to
reprobate aristocratic vice ; to be meek, yet outspoken ;
to be simple, yet quick-witted ; to be innocent, yet wide-
awake and on her guard. It would seem almost impossible
that Richardson should succeed in steering so intricate a
path. But each incident is related with such careful attention to detail, Pamela's letters give so powerful a sense of
immediacy, and Richardson himself preserves such an un-
hesitating belief in Pamela's word and in the truth of appear-

ances, that almost he would persuade us to believe too. Almost, but not quite. Many contemporaries were persuaded ; but others saw that a different interpretation was possible, and amongst these was Fielding.

To convey this alternative interpretation, Fielding called upon his experience in burlesque and produced, pseudonymously, *An Apology for the Life of Mrs. Shamela Andrews. In which, the many notorious Falshoods and Misrepresentations of a book called Pamela, are Exposed and refuted ; and all the matchless Arts of that young Politician, set in a true and just Light. Together with A full Account of all that passed between her and Parson Arthur Williams ; whose Character is represented in a manner something different from that which he bears in Pamela. The whole being exact Copies of authentick Papers delivered to the Editor.* It is a riotous travesty, in which Pamela is shown as a shameless and designing hussy, yet ready to talk for ' a full Hour and a half, about my Vartue' or ' of honourable Designs till Supper-time ', and Mr. B's full name is discovered to be Booby. And just as the rehearsed plays in *Pasquin* and *The Historical Register* had been enclosed within a framework of commentary from the supposed author and his friend, so these authentic letters are sent to Parson Tickletext, who had taken *Pamela* at Richardson's valuation, by Parson Oliver who knew the facts.

If any moral is to be drawn, it is that the distinction between being and seeming must be recognized. No exponent of the comedy of manners could fail to draw such a distinction, and Fielding's plays are especially rich in characters who are not what they seem, from Lady Gravely, the affected prude of *The Temple Beau*, to the false and grasping Valences of *The Fathers*. But Fielding had more than a professional dramatist's interest in unmasking appearances. He returned to the subject in an essay on the Pursuit of Reputation, published in *The Champion*, 4 March 1740, where he showed that folly and vice ' are continually industrious to disguise themselves ', and wear the habits of virtue and wisdom; ' which the world, always judging by the outside, easily suffers them to accomplish'; and the irony of *The Life of Mr. Jonathan Wild the Great* is sustained—tediously, it must be admitted—to prove that the Great Man, properly considered, is no better than a gangster.

The distinction between being and seeming is the guiding principle of *Joseph Andrews*. In the preface to his novel Fielding explains that the Ridiculous is his province, that the only source of the true Ridiculous is Affectation, and that Affectation 'proceeds from one of these two causes, Vanity or Hypocrisy'. To display the Ridiculous he has devised this new kind of writing, the comic epic poem in prose, observing the best epic practice in such matters as fable and characters ; but whereas the epic fable is customarily grave and solemn, his will be light and ridiculous, and whereas epic characters are of the highest, his will mostly be of inferior rank and manners. The difficulty is to see how Fielding interprets the representation of the fable in action. Fortunately he is more explicit in the preface he wrote for his sister's novel, *David Simple* (1744). There, after referring to his preface to *Joseph Andrews*, he mentions the two great originals of all epic writing, the *Iliad* and the *Odyssey*, which

> differ principally in the action, which in the *Iliad* is entire and uniform ; in the *Odyssey*, is rather a series of actions, all tending to produce one great end.

The followers of Homer have all observed this principal difference, whether their imitations were serious or comic ; and so we see that just as Pope in *The Dunciad* fixed on one action, Butler and Cervantes fixed on a series. His sister's work belongs to the latter category:

> the fable consists of a series of separate adventures, detached from and independent on each other, yet all tending to one great end.

The same may also be seen in *Joseph Andrews*. That also is an Odysseyan epic, 'consisting of a series of separate adventures, detached from and independent on each other, yet all tending to one great end '; and it may be observed that just as the *Odyssey* relates the adventures of Odysseus in finding his way home and the hardships which befell him after incurring the wrath of Poseidon, so Fielding relates the adventures of Joseph Andrews and Parson Adams in finding their way home and the hardships which befell them after Joseph had incurred the wrath of Lady Booby. Perhaps contemporary readers might have noticed an even closer application of the burlesque. The critic Ramsay had pointed out that in Fénelon's *Aventures de Télémaque* it is the hatred of Venus rather than the wrath of Poseidon that supplies the cause of the action, and that ' the Hatred of *Venus* against a young Prince, that despises Pleasure for the Sake of Virtue, and subdues his Passions by the Assistance of Wisdom, is a Fable drawn from Nature, and at the same Time includes the sublimest Morality '. No reader could fail to relish the notion of the lascivious Lady Booby in the role of Venus, whose desire for her handsome footman Joseph Andrews is turned to hatred when that young Prince despises Pleasure for the sake of Virtue, and subdues his passions by the assistance of his sister Pamela's wisdom.

But what is the great end to which all the separate adventures are tending ? Why, surely, the display of the Ridiculous, of those affectations which arise from vanity and hypocrisy. This is the characteristic common to Lady Booby, Mrs. Slipslop, and Mrs. Grave-airs, all of them women who pretend to more modesty, more learning, or more gentility than they possess. And this is the characteristic of the innkeepers and their wives who can make a show of human kindness once they are satisfied of the standing of their guests, of the soldiers who pretend to valour, of the justices who pretend to a knowledge of the law, and of the parsons who pretend to godliness. Even Parson Trulliber can make a show of Methodism, when he is satisfied that Adams has not come to buy his pigs : ' Get out of my doors ', he cries, when Adams tells him that, in addition to faith, he must perform the good works of giving to the needy ; ' Fellow, dost thou speak against faith in my house ? I will no longer remain under the same roof with a wretch who speaks wantonly of faith and the Scriptures.'

The two interpolated stories fall into place in this pattern. The Unfortunate Jilt is a story of pretence to affection, and the story of Mr. Wilson is a tale of the pretences practised in London life. Vanity of vanities is Mr. Wilson's theme as he recalls his experiences of life in the Temple amongst smart fellows who drank with lords they did not know and intrigued with women they never saw ; and of town coquettes animated solely by vanity who sometimes have a whim to affect wisdom, wit, good-nature, politeness, and health, but are also affected to put on ugliness, folly, nonsense, ill-nature, ill-breeding, and sickness in their turns.

Such are Mr. Wilson's reflexions. Far from being an idle digression, they are highly appropriate to Fielding's scheme and purpose ; for his action, by confining him to the high road and the inn, precludes him from commenting upon London life, and it is a sample of London society which Mr. Wilson's story exposes.

But these at worst are transient characters, and at best they are minor. What of Parson Adams himself ? He too has his vanities, innocent vanities indeed, of his learning and his power as a preacher. His role however is that of a modern Don Quixote ; a man of good sense, good parts, and good nature, as Fielding declares, but ' as entirely ignorant of the ways of this world as an infant just entered into it could possibly be '. His book-reading did not, like his illustrious prototype's, lead him to mistake windmills for giants or inns for castles ; it led him instead to expect on every hand an honest, undesigning, Christian behaviour. He is therefore constantly the victim of deceit. But he never loses our affection, partly because his expectations are noble, and partly because (like Don Quixote again) he hurls himself upon the oppressor thinking only of the blows his two fists or his crabstick will deliver, and nothing of those he will receive. It is not merely in such episodes as the fight at the inn which interrupts the story of The Unfortunate

Jilt, or the 'roasting' of Adams by the fox-hunting squire (which recalls the treatment of Don Quixote at the hands of the Duke and Duchess), or the midnight tussle with Mrs. Slipslop where Adams believes himself bewitched, that the reader recognizes the justice of the assertion on the title-page of *Joseph Andrews*, that it is ' Written in Imitation of the Manner of Cervantes '.

But there are two sides to the relationship of being and seeming. While most of the men and women we meet in *Joseph Andrews* are worse than they seem, others are better. And though the bedraggled appearance of the worthy Adams is the most prominent example, Fielding asks us to notice that the man who pays the stranded travellers' bill is not the wealthy Parson Trulliber but 'a fellow who had been formerly a drummer in an Irish regiment, and now travelled the country as a pedlar '; that when Joseph lies sick at the Tow-wouses' inn, it is not the surgeon, or the parson, or the innkeeper, who looks after him, but Betty the chambermaid, whose morals are no better than they should be ; and when Joseph has been found wounded and naked in a ditch, it is not any of the fine ladies in a passing coach who takes pity on him, but the postilion,

> (a lad who hath been since transported for robbing a hen-roost), [who] voluntarily stript off a greatcoat, his only garment, at the same time swearing a great oath (for which he was rebuked by the passengers), ' that he would rather ride in his shirt all his life than suffer a fellow-creature to lie in so miserable a condition '.

To some extent, this anatomy of the ridiculous is a counterblast to *Pamela*, and by recalling certain incidents in that novel and introducing one or two of its characters, Fielding made sure that we should keep *Pamela* in view. Richardson had placed an implicit trust in the truth of appearances. But that way lies self-deception : it is only by the most careful scrutiny that we can see beneath appearances and find the true springs of human action.

IV

Yet appearances are important too. ' It is not enough ',
Fielding writes, ' that your designs, nay that your actions,
are intrinsically good ; you must take care that they shall
appear so '; for ' prudence and circumspection are necessary even to the best of men '. The passage occurs in one
of those chapters of *Tom Jones* (III, 7) ' in which the author
himself makes his appearance on the stage ', and it is close
to the heart of the novel. The theme is in fact announced
in similar terms in the Dedication :

> I have endeavoured strongly to inculcate, that virtue and
> innocence can scarce ever be injured but by indiscretion ; and
> . . . it is this alone which often betrays them into the snares
> which deceit and villany spread for them.

To illustrate this Fielding chose a hero as typical of his order
of society as the epic hero was of his. We are asked to recognize that Tom, in spite of some lack of prudence and
circumspection, and in spite of some contraventions of the
moral code, is essentially a good man. It might be said of
Tom as Ramsay had said of Fénelon's Telemachus:

> Our Poet does not lift *Telemachus* above Humanity ; he
> makes him fall into such Weaknesses, as are compatible with a
> sincere Love of Virtue.

Young Mr. Blifil, on the other hand, with whom Tom is
brought up in Mr. Allworthy's household, has more than
enough of prudence and circumspection, but his love of
virtue is on a par with the affectations which Fielding exposed
in *Joseph Andrews*. The distinction is one which Sheridan
was to familiarize when he contrasted the brothers Charles
and Joseph Surface in *The School for Scandal*.

The best critical theory of the day was agreed that an epic
should have a beginning, a middle, and an end, that the beginning should deal with the causes of the action, and that in
the causes might be observed two opposite ' designs ', the
hero's and the design of those who opposed him. In

adopting these sensible precepts, Fielding provided an intro-
ductory section of six books in which numerous incidents
open Tom's character and reveal the designs of Blifil and
his two tutors, Thwackum and Square, who sought to
prejudice Tom in the eyes of Mr. Allworthy and to prevent
him from marrying Sophia and inheriting Squire Western's
estate. Tom is shown (IV, 6) to have ' somewhat about
him, which, though I think writers are not thoroughly
agreed in its name ' (the philosopher Shaftesbury had called
it the ' moral sense ')

> . . . doth certainly inhabit some human breasts; whose use is
> not so properly to distinguish right from wrong, as to prompt
> and incite them to the former, and to restrain and withhold
> them from the latter. . . . Though he did not always act
> rightly, yet he never did otherwise without feeling and suffering
> for it.

Thus the boy is incited to sell the little horse which Mr. Allworthy had given him so as to prevent the family of a dismissed servant from starving, and he is prompted to risk
his neck in recovering Sophia's pet bird which Blifil had
maliciously allowed to escape. And if as a young man he
is also prompted to fornication with the gamekeeper's
daughter, he is prepared to deal honourably with her until
he discovers that he was not the first to seduce her ; and if
he was drunk and disorderly in Mr. Allworthy's house, it
was because he had already been thrown into an ' immoder-
ate excess of rapture ' on hearing that Mr. Allworthy was
recovering from his dangerous illness. Allworthy sum-
marizes (V, 7) what Fielding wishes us to think of Tom,
when he says to him on his sickbed :

> I am convinced, my child, that you have much goodness,
> generosity, and honour, in your temper : if you will add pru-
> dence and religion to these, you must be happy.

But in spite of his conviction, Allworthy allows his mind
to be poisoned by the malicious insinuations of Blifil, and
turns Tom away from his house into a series of adventures on

the high road, corresponding to those of Joseph Andrews and Parson Adams. They fill the second six books of the novel and correspond, in epic terms, to ' the Shipping off of Æneas, his Voyages, his Battels, and all the Obstacles he met with ', which (in the words of Le Bossu, the chief authority on epic structure at that time) ' compose a just Middle ; [for] they are a Consequence of the Destruction of Troy . . . and these same Incidents require an End '.

The high road led to London, and on it are not only Tom (and Partridge, his Sancho Panza) but Sophia, who has fled from her father's house to escape being forced into marriage with Blifil. As in *Joseph Andrews*, the high road and the inn provide a suitable scene for the testing of character, the recognition of bad nature masquerading as good, and of good nature concealed or tainted by imprudence. Tom has something to learn even from the Man of the Hill who, like Mr. Wilson and like many a character in epic, is permitted to interrupt the narrative with his story. The Man of the Hill provides further instances of imprudence, in particular of incautiousness in placing his affections, and as a result he had become a misanthrope and a hermit. But, as Tom permits himself to comment (VIII, 15), ' What better could be expected in love derived from the stews, or in friendship first produced and nourished at the gaming table ?' One must not think evil of the rest of mankind on that account, for, as Tom continues, enunciating Fielding's doctrines of the Good-Natured Man and the deceptiveness of appearances:

> If there was, indeed, much more wickedness in the world than there is, it would not prove such general assertions against human nature, since much of this arrives by mere accident, and many a man who commits evil is not totally bad and corrupt in his heart.

Sophia too is learning as much as Tom, directly in such scenes as that at the inn at Upton, and by proxy as she listens to Mrs. Fitzpatrick's cautionary tale of her imprudent mar-

riage, interrupted as it is by appeals to Sophia to declare how
she would have acted in like circumstances.

The lovers reach London independently and the final
section of six further books begins. Tom's good nature is
as clear as ever, notably in his generous treatment of the
highwayman who was driven by penury to attack him, and
in his chivalrous championship of Mrs. Miller's daughter ;
but alas, his imprudence is clearer still in ' the ignominious
circumstance of being kept ' by Lady Bellaston. Fielding
never asks his readers to overlook Tom's misdemeanours.
His worst offence is most severely punished, for his relations
with Lady Bellaston cannot be forgiven by Sophia ; and
we see him at the end of the Sixteenth Book at the nadir of
his fortunes, rejected by Sophia, dismissed from Allworthy's
favour, and imprisoned on a charge of murdering his oppo-
nent in a duel. ' Such ', Fielding muses (XVII, 1), ' are
the calamities in which he is at present involved, owing to
his imprudence . . . that we almost despair of bringing him
to any good ; and if our reader delights in seeing executions,
I think he ought not to lose any time in taking a first row at
Tyburn.' Readers of the epic will recognize that the time
is ripe for a Discovery or a Reversal of Fortune, perhaps even
for both, and they will recall that it was not unusual for the
author to invoke divine aid for rescuing a hero in distress.
Fielding has prepared both for his Discovery—that was
allowed for in making Tom a foundling—and for his
Reversal of Fortune ; but he disdains to employ the marvellous. It is true that luck is on Tom's side when his victim
in the duel recovers from his wound, and when the facts of
his parentage (concealed by Blifil) are discovered ; but in
other respects the reader is asked to recognize that Tom has
worked his passage. He has cast his bread upon the waters
in acts of abundant good nature, and by the assistance of
Mrs. Miller's representations to Mr. Allworthy he finds it
after many days. His Virtue is Rewarded by restoration
into the favour of Allworthy and the good graces of Sophia.
Since he is now discovered to be Allworthy's nephew and

heir, Squire Western has no further objections to bestowing his daughter upon him ; they marry, and ' preserve the purest and tenderest affection for each other, an affection daily increased and confirmed by mutual endearments, and mutual esteem '.

This is a pious hope which the reader may find it difficult to share, for it rests upon the large assumption that Tom had ceased to be indiscreet. Furthermore he was at best a good-natured man ; and though endowed with a well-developed Moral Sense, he required on Allworthy's evidence to add religion as well as prudence to his good nature. Even if we allow that he had become prudent, there is nothing to show that he had become religious. Some such reflexions seem to have occurred to Fielding, for his next novel, *Amelia* (1752), begins where *Tom Jones* leaves off. Captain and Mrs. Booth also entertained the purest and tenderest affection for each other and confirmed it by mutual endearments and mutual esteem, yet various accidents befell them owing partly to Booth's character, and it is with these accidents and with their effect upon this worthy couple that the novel is concerned.

V

The decision to deal with the accidents of domestic life set Fielding some new problems in structure. The high road and the inn could have no place here since married folk are not usually nomadic, and consequently we miss the Odyssean–Quixotic episodes which provided him in the earlier novels with so many shining opportunities for un-masking affectation and testing character. He had also to decide how to relate the earlier history of his couple, a prob-lem he had not been required to face before. But the comic adaptation of epic conventions was ready to hand here as it had been at the beginning of *Joseph Andrews*. Just as Æneas was stranded on the coasts of Carthage, was succoured there by Dido, related to her his story, and consummated his furtive love in a cave, so Captain Booth was stranded in

Newgate Prison, was succoured there by Miss Matthews, a
high-class courtesan, related to her his story, and consummated his furtive love in a superior kind of cell.   Nor is this
merely an ingenious piece of burlesque.   Booth's misde-
meanour with Miss Matthews, which he is ashamed to con-
fess to Amelia, dogs him throughout the novel ; while the
sombreness of the opening scenes in Newgate Prison set
the tone of the book.   Fielding takes care to show us the
squalor and oppression which is the lot of the penniless
prisoner, and on the other hand the relative comfort which
is to be had at the price of a bribe ; and he describes the
coarse and depraved ruffians, male and female, the tricksters
and sharpers, who molest and prey upon the weak, the unfortunate, and even the innocent, who have come there
through a miscarriage of justice.   This is the scene in which
we first discover Booth, whose previous history shows
him to be imprudent, liable to deception, with ' very slight
and uncertain' notions of religion, yet essentially good-
natured.   He will not return to Newgate, but he will always
be in danger of return.   And when he escapes, the reader
recognizes that Newgate was only a somewhat more lurid
epitome of society outside, where merit counts for nothing,
where civil and military places go by influence exerted for
a bribe, where those in high place have rogues, pimps, and
bawds in their pay, and where gallantry is a cover for fornication and adultery.   Fielding had said as much long ago in
his play *The Modern Husband* (1731), and had repeated it in
Jonathan Wild ; and if *Joseph Andrews* and *Tom Jones* appear
lighter in tone than *Amelia*, it is only because the scene is
laid more frequently in the country.   London is the breed-
ing place for such creatures as Lord Fellamar and Lady
Bellaston, and Mr. Wilson anticipated Booth in finding that
in London ' poverty and distress, with their horrid trains of
duns, attorneys, bailiffs, haunted me day and night.   My
clothes grew shabby, my credit bad, my friends and acquaintance of all kinds cold.'
    The scene is in fact so sombre that a tragic conclusion

seems inevitable.   Even a stronger and a better man than
Booth could scarcely escape that fate.   In considering the
conclusion to which he was leading his ' worthy couple ',
Fielding is likely to have paid attention to the best critical
teaching available.   The consensus of opinion amongst com-
mentators upon the epic pointed to a conclusion favour-
able to the hero.   Le Bossu indeed could discover no reason
why that should be so;

> ' yet if any heed be given to Authority,' he concluded, ' I do
> not know any one Instance of a Poet, who finishes his Piece
> with the Misfortunes of his Heroe. . . .   The *Epick Poem*'s
> Action is of a larger Extent than that of the Theatre ; [and] it
> would perhaps be less satisfactory to the Reader, if, after so
> much Pains and so long Troubles with which this kind of Poem
> is always fill'd, it should at last bring them to a doleful and
> unhappy End.'

The easiest way of bringing the Booths to a happy end
might well have been to repeat the formula of *Tom Jones*
and show the eventual reward of the hero's virtuous actions.
But Fielding seems to have been no longer content with such
teaching.   It was Booth's mistake to believe that as men
' act entirely from their passions, their actions can have
neither merit nor demerit '.   If a man's ruling passion happened to be benevolence, he would relieve the distress of
others ;   but if it were avarice, ambition, or pride, other
men's miseries would have no effect upon him.   Booth
is eventually to be corrected of an error, which to Amelia
seemed little better than atheism, by reading a volume of
Barrow's sermons while detained in the bailiff's house ; but
in the meanwhile Fielding allows him little opportunity for
charity.   The reader notices instead how his imprudence in
the use of what little money he has reduces Amelia to penury,
and how his ill-placed trust and his single act of fornication endangers her chastity.   She, however, shows herself
to be on all occasions a model of wifely prudence, constancy,
obedience, forgiveness, and love.

' To retrieve the ill consequences of a foolish conduct, and
by struggling manfully with distress to subdue it, is one of
the noblest efforts of wisdom and virtue.' That is all that
Fielding asks of his worthy couple ; and having displayed
their struggles, he is not averse to rescuing them by an Epic
Discovery (that Amelia is an heiress) and an Epic Reversal
of Fortune, which enables a now prudent and Christian
Booth to retire to a country estate.

In *Amelia*, as in *Tom Jones*, Fielding infers that at the end
of the book the hero is in some respects an altered man
without persuading us of the fact. Dickens was the first
novelist to succeed in such persuasion and George Eliot the
first to specialize in showing the modifying effect of incident
upon character. These Victorian successes have made de-
mands which the modern reader is inclined to impose both
upon earlier novelists and earlier dramatists without perhaps reflecting whether changes in character are altogether
necessary or always important. *Amelia*, like *Tom Jones*,
deals with wider issues than the modification of character.
It has to do not merely with Booth and his wife, but with
miseries and distresses typical of mid-eighteenth century
London life. No other novel provides such a wide panor-
ama of London society or better conveys what it was like to
live in London in the seventeen-fifties.

VI

In a paper which he wrote for the last of his periodicals,
The Covent Garden Journal (28 January 1752), Fielding declared that he would not trouble the world with any more
novels. He had not been entirely committed to the pro-
fession of letters since the abrupt termination of his dramatic
career. The severity of his attack upon Walpole's govern-
ment in *Pasquin* had led directly to the Licensing Act of 1737
and to the closure of all theatres but Drury Lane and Covent
Garden. Fielding's Little Theatre in the Haymarket was
the principal victim, and his chief source of income was thus

removed.   He thereupon began a serious study of the law, was called to the bar in 1740, and practised for some time on the Western Circuit.   Shortly after completing *Tom Jones* in 1748, and before its publication, he had been appointed a police-court magistrate at Bow Street, and his jurisdiction was soon extended to the whole of the County of Middlesex. As a magistrate he was exceptionally industrious, and did much to break up the gangs of thieves which infested London.   His *Enquiry Into the Causes of the late Increase of Robbers* (1751), dedicated to Lord Chancellor Hardwicke, shows both an extensive knowledge of the law, and an intimate acquaintance with the evil and its origin.   His energies might have been directed more and more to clearing up the criminal underworld if his health had not broken down.   In the summer of 1754 he undertook a sea trip to Lisbon with his wife and daughter in a desperate search for health, and whiled away his time in keeping a dairy.   This he revised, and the manuscript was posthumously published as *A Journal of a Voyage to Lisbon*.   Not the least of its merits is the picture it gives us of the man himself, affectionately considerate to his family, patiently suffering from an incurable disease, yet observing with undiminished zest the oddities of human behaviour, and seizing such opportunities as incidents offered for social or political comment.   The book is prefaced by a disquisition on travel literature comparable in kind to the disquisition on the comic epic poem in prose which prefaces *Joseph Andrews*.   Once again Fielding declared that he was laying down the rules for a kind of writing which had not been properly undertaken before (except by Lord Anson in the published account of his circumnavigation, 1740-44) ; for travellers seem to have fallen either into the fault of ' filling their pages with monsters which nobody hath ever seen, and with adventures which never have, nor could possibly have happened to them ', or on the other hand they

   waste their time and paper with recording things and facts of so common a kind, that they challenge no other right of being remembered than as they had the honour of having happened to the author.

This opportunity of reforming travel literature was as haphazard as the chance he took of reforming the novel, but even if he had lived longer—he died on 8 October 1754 at the age of forty-seven—it was not likely that he would have had occasion to write more in this kind. It is easy, however, to see that his theories might have been profitably applied to biography, and that he was well equipped by imagination, a reverence for truth, judgement, and a sense of proportion to succeed in that kindred form.

But this is idle speculation. Even though he may have felt that he had outgrown the novel, it is there that his achievement lies ; and it is an achievement typical of an age which relished the mock-epics of Pope and the ballad operas of Gay. Like those poets Fielding brought literary experience gained in other writing and a wealth of critical learning to bear upon the production of a new form, but a form which constantly recalls older, well-tried forms and adapts them to the spirit and use of his own times ; and he used this form to display ' just copies of human manners ' and to offer ' lectures of conduct, and introductions into life '.

FIELDING

A Select Bibliography

(Place of publication London, unless stated otherwise)

Collected Editions:

THE WORKS, 4 vols.   Edited by Arthur Murphy (1762).

THE DRAMATIC WORKS, 4 vols. (1783).

THE WORKS, 10 vols.   Edited by Alexander Chalmers (1806).

THE WORKS.   Edited by Thomas Roscoe (1840).

THE WORKS, 10 vols.   Edited by Leslie Stephen (1882).

THE WORKS, 12 vols.   Edited by George Saintsbury (1893).

THE WORKS, 12 vols.   Edited by Edmund Gosse (1899).

THE COMPLETE WORKS, 16 vols.   Edited by W. E. Henley and others (1903).

Selections:

MISCELLANIES, 3 vols. (1743).
   [Vol. 1 contains poems and essays; Vol. 2, *A Journey from this World to the Next* and plays; Vol. 3, *The Life of Mr. Jonathan Wild the Great.*]

THE BEAUTIES OF FIELDING (1782).

MISCELLANIES AND POEMS.   Edited by James P. Browne (1872).

SELECTED ESSAYS.   Edited by Gordon Hall Gerould.   New York (1905).

FIELDING.   Edited by George Saintsbury (1909).

FIELDING.   Edited by L. Rice-Oxley.   Oxford (1923).

Collected Novels:

THE NOVELS.   Edited by Sir Walter Scott (1821).

THE NOVELS.   Edited by Thomas Roscoe (1831-2).

THE WORKS.   Edited by George Saintsbury (1926).

FIELDING'S NOVELS, 10 vols.   Oxford (1926).

Separate Editions of the Novels:

THE HISTORY OF THE ADVENTURES OF JOSEPH ANDREWS AND OF HIS
FRIEND MR. ABRAHAM ADAMS, 2 vols. (1742).
[Edited by J. Paul de Castro (1929). The Everyman Library
edition (1910) contains a preface by George Saintsbury, the
World's Classics edition (1929) one by L. Rice-Oxley.]

THE LIFE OF MR. JONATHAN WILD THE GREAT (1743).
[First published in *Miscellanies. A New Edition with considerable
corrections and additions*, 1754. The World's Classics edition
(1951) reprints the text of 1743 with the variants of 1754 in an
appendix.]

THE HISTORY OF TOM JONES, A FOUNDLING, 6 vols. (1749).
[The Everyman Library edition (2 vols., 1909) has an introduc-
tion by George Saintsbury.]

AMELIA, 4 vols. (1752).
[Fielding's revised text was first published in Murphy's edition
of the Works. The Everyman Library edition has an intro-
duction by George Saintsbury.]

Plays:

LOVE IN SEVERAL MASQUES, A COMEDY (1728).

THE TEMPLE BEAU, A COMEDY (1730).

THE AUTHOR'S FARCE (1730).

TOM THUMB, A TRAGEDY (1730).
[A revised edition with annotations, entitled *The Tragedy of
Tragedies; or the Life and Death of Tom Thumb the Great*, was
published in 1731. Both texts are reprinted in J. T. Hillhouse's
edition, New Haven, 1918.]

RAPE UPON RAPE; OR, THE JUSTICE CAUGHT IN HIS OWN TRAP, A
COMEDY (1730).

THE LETTER-WRITERS: OR, A NEW WAY TO KEEP A WIFE AT HOME,
A FARCE (1731).

THE WELSH OPERA: OR, THE GREY MARE THE BETTER HORSE (1731).

THE LOTTERY, A FARCE (1732).

THE MODERN HUSBAND, A COMEDY (1732).

THE OLD DEBAUCHEES, A COMEDY (1732).

THE COVENT-GARDEN TRAGEDY (1732).

THE MOCK DOCTOR, OR THE DUMB LADY CUR'D.   A COMEDY, DONE
FROM MOLIERE (1732).

THE MISER.   A COMEDY, TAKEN FROM PLAUTUS AND MOLIERE (1733).

THE INTRIGUING CHAMBERMAID, A COMEDY (1734).

DON QUIXOTE IN ENGLAND, A COMEDY (1734).
[Contains the famous songs *When Mighty roast beef was the
Englishman's food* and *The dusky night rides down the sky*.]

AN OLD MAN TAUGHT WISDOM: OR, THE VIRGIN UNMASK'D, A
FARCE (1735).

THE UNIVERSAL GALLANT : OR, THE DIFFERENT HUSBANDS, A COMEDY
(1735).

PASQUIN, A DRAMATICK SATIRE ON THE TIMES (1736).

TUMBLE-DOWN DICK: OR, PHAETON IN THE SUDS.   A DRAMATICK
ENTERTAINMENT (1736).

EURYDICE, A FARCE (1737).

THE HISTORICAL REGISTER FOR THE YEAR 1736 (1737).
[Also contains *Eurydice Hiss'd*, ' a very merry Tragedy '.]

MISS LUCY IN TOWN, A FARCE (1742).

THE WEDDING-DAY, A COMEDY (1743).

THE FATHERS : OR, THE GOOD-NATUR'D MAN, A COMEDY (1778).

Other Writings:

THE CHAMPION, 15 November 1739–19 June 1740; 2 vols., 1741.

OF TRUE GREATNESS (1741).

THE VERNONIAD (1741).

AN APOLOGY FOR THE LIFE OF MRS. SHAMELA ANDREWS (1741).
[Reprinted with essays by R. Brimley Johnson (1926), Brian
W. Downs (1930), and Sheridan W. Baker, Jr., Berkeley (1953).]

THE CRISIS, A SERMON (1741).

THE OPPOSITION, A VISION (1742).

A FULL VINDICATION OF THE DUTCHESS DOWAGER OF MARLBOROUGH
(1742).

PLUTUS, THE GOD OF RICHES. A COMEDY, TRANSLATED FROM THE ORIGINAL GREEK OF ARISTOPHANES (1742).

SOME PAPERS PROPER TO BE READ BEFORE THE ROYAL SOCIETY (1743).

A SERIOUS ADDRESS TO THE PEOPLE OF GREAT BRITAIN (1745).

A DIALOGUE BETWEEN THE DEVIL, THE POPE, AND THE PRETENDER (1745).

THE TRUE PATRIOT, 5 November 1745–17 June 1746.

OVID'S ART OF LOVE PARAPHRASED (1747).

THE JACOBITE'S JOURNAL, 5 December 1747–5 November 1748.

A CHARGE DELIVERED TO THE GRAND JURY (1749).

A TRUE STATE OF THE CASE OF BOSAVERN PENLEZ (1749).

AN ENQUIRY INTO THE CAUSES OF THE LATE INCREASE OF ROBBERS (1751).

A PLAN OF THE UNIVERSAL REGISTER OFFICE (1752).

THE COVENT-GARDEN JOURNAL, 4 January–25 November 1752. [Edited by G. E. Jensen, 2 vols., New Haven (1915).]

EXAMPLES OF THE INTERPOSITION OF PROVIDENCE IN THE DETECTION AND PUNISHMENT OF MURDER (1752).

A PROPOSAL FOR MAKING AN EFFECTUAL PROVISION FOR THE POOR (1753).

A CLEAR STATE OF THE CASE OF ELIZABETH CANNING (1753).

THE JOURNAL OF A VOYAGE TO LISBON (1755). [A full edition was published the same year and suppressed. There are editions by Austin Dobson (1892, 1907), and J. H. Lobban (1913). It is reprinted with *Jonathan Wild* in Everyman's Library.]

Some Critical and Biographical Studies:

LECTURES ON THE ENGLISH COMIC WRITERS. By William Hazlitt (1819).

LIVES OF THE NOVELISTS. By Sir Walter Scott (1825).

THE ENGLISH HUMOURISTS OF THE EIGHTEENTH CENTURY. By W. M. Thackeray (1853).

FIELDING. By Austin Dobson (1883).

EIGHTEENTH CENTURY VIGNETTES. By Austin Dobson (1st ser. 1892; 2nd ser. 1896).

THE ENGLISH NOVEL. By Sir Walter Raleigh (1894).

HENRY FIELDING: A MEMOIR. By G. M. Godden (1910).

THE HISTORY OF HENRY FIELDING. By Wilbur L. Cross. 3 vols., New Haven (1910).
[The standard biography, with valuable bibliography.]

LES ROMANS DE FIELDING. Par Aurélien Digeon. Paris (1923).
[An English translation appeared in 1925.]

FIELDING THE NOVELIST. By Frederic T. Blanchard. New Haven (1926).
[A study in Fielding's reputation.]

ENGLISH COMIC DRAMA, 1700–1750. By F. W. Bateson. Oxford (1929).

HENRY FIELDING'S THEORY OF THE COMIC PROSE EPIC. By Ethel M. Thornbury. Madison (1931).

FIELDING'S THEORY OF THE NOVEL. By Frederick O. Bissell. Ithaca (1933).

HENRY FIELDING, NOVELIST AND MAGISTRATE. By B. M. Jones (1933).

THE ENGLISH COUNTRY SQUIRE AS DEPICTED IN ENGLISH PROSE FICTION FROM 1740 TO 1800. By Kenneth Chester Slagle. Philadelphia (1938).

THE MAKING OF JONATHAN WILD. By W. R. Irwin. New York (1941).

A TRUE BORN ENGLISHMAN: BEING THE LIFE OF HENRY FIELDING. By M. P. Willcocks (1947).

HENRY FIELDING. By Elizabeth Jenkins (1947).

HENRY FIELDING: HIS LIFE, WORKS, AND TIMES. By F. Homes Dudden. 2 vols., Oxford (1952).
[Useful on the social background.]

NOTE: Fielding's *Amelia*: an interpretation, by George Sherburn, *E.L.H.*, A Journal of English Literary History, Vol. 3, 1936, is an outstanding essay.